D1607301

Apatosaurus

BY BARBARA ALPERT

amicus
high interest

Amicus High Interest is published by Amicus
P.O. Box 1329, Mankato, MN 56002
www.amicuspublishing.us

Library of Congress Cataloging-in-Publication Data
Alpert, Barbara.
  Apatosaurus / by Barbara Alpert.
     pages cm. -- (Digging for dinosaurs)
  Audience: K to grade 3
  Summary: "Describes how the Apatosaurus was discovered,
how paleontologists study its bones, and what the fossil
evidence tells us about dinosaur behavior"-- Provided by
publisher.
  Includes bibliographical references and index.
  ISBN 978-1-60753-365-8 (library binding)
  1. Apatosaurus--Juvenile literature. I. Title.
  QE862.S3A435 2014
  567.913'8--dc23
                                        2012035410

Editor   Rebecca Glaser
Series Designer   Kathleen Petelinsek
Page production   Red Line Editorial, Inc.

Photo Credits
Shutterstock Images, cover; DEA Picture Library/Getty
Images, 5; Ryan Brocklehurst/iStockphoto, 6; North
Wind/North Wind Picture Archives, 8; 123RF, 11; Joyce
Photographics/Science Source, 12; Field Museum Library/
Getty Images, 15; Steve Geer/iStockphoto, 16; Jim
Jurica/iStockphoto, 19; Dorling Kindersley RF/Thinkstock,
20; Francois Gohier/Science Source, 23; De Agostini/
SuperStock, 24; dieKleinert/Alamy, 26; Robert Harding
Picture Library/SuperStock, 28

Printed in the United States of America at Corporate Graphics
in North Mankato, Minnesota
5-2013 / P.O. 1148.
10 9 8 7 6 5 4 3 2 1

Table of Contents

What is an Apatosaurus?

Apatosaurus walked next to a forest. There was so much to eat. With dull teeth, it grabbed leaves off trees. It broke off a branch and swallowed it whole. Then it lifted its long neck. Now the dinosaur could reach the treetops.

Apatosaurus munched on
leaves from the tops of trees.

Scientists think Apatosaurus held its tail up when it walked.

 Q How do we know how Apatosaurus walked?

Apatosaurus was more than 70 feet (21 m) long. That's as long as two school buses. Its tail was longer than its neck. Its legs were like tree trunks. It moved like an elephant, walking with straight legs. It kept its tail up.

 Scientists study **fossils** of footprints. They are called "**trackways**." Scientists did not find tail marks with Apatosaurus prints.

O.C. Marsh was the paleontologist who got to name Apatosaurus.

8

The Discovery of Apatosaurus

In 1877, Arthur Lakes found a fossil bone in Colorado. It was so big he couldn't take it home by himself. Then he found more huge bones. Lakes wrote to a **paleontologist** named O.C. Marsh. Marsh worked at the Peabody Museum at Yale. The bones were sent to him.

Marsh studied the bones. The tailbones looked like the bones of **mosasaurs**. A mosasaur was a sea reptile. But these bones were different. It was a new dinosaur! So Marsh named it Apatosaurus, or "**deceptive** lizard." This means it could fool you. It almost fooled Marsh!

 Why did Marsh get to name Apatosaurus?

**A mosaasaur was a lizard
that could swim.**

 The first scientist to discover a dinosaur gets to
name it.

Some Apatosaurus bones were too big for one person to carry.

 **Q** Why was Brontosaurus named after thunder?

Marsh sent men to look for more bones. In 1879, they found a **skeleton**. It looked just like the Apatosaurus. But it was bigger! Marsh studied both of them. Apatosaurus had three bones at the end of its **spine**. The new one had five. So Marsh thought they were two different dinosaurs. Marsh named the new one Brontosaurus, or "thunder lizard."

 It was so big that it must have sounded like thunder when it walked.

Scientists studied the bones more. Elmer Riggs worked at the Field Museum of Chicago. In 1903, he showed that Apatosaurus and Brontosaurus were the same. Brontosaurus was older. That is why it had extra bones in its spine. Apatosaurus was a young Brontosaurus. But Apatosaurus was named first. So that made it the official name.

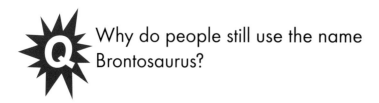

Q Why do people still use the name Brontosaurus?

Elmer Riggs (right) realized the two dinosaurs were the same.

 Books, articles, and museums used the name for years. "Thunder lizard" seems like a better name for this huge dinosaur.

For years, no one knew what kind of head Apatosaurus had.

Q Why are dinosaur skulls hard to find?

Piecing it Together

No one knew what kind of head
Apatosaurus had. No skulls had been
found. But Marsh wanted to show his
skeleton at the museum. So he made
a copy of a big, round Camarasaurus
skull. In 1909, Earl Douglass dug up an
Apatosaurus with a skull. But it seemed
too small. So he put the skeleton together
without a skull.

 Dinosaur leg bones and backbones are heavy.
They can survive being buried. Dinosaur skulls
are not as tough. Many break into pieces.

In 1936, scientists at the Carnegie Museum put a skull on Apatosaurus. The skull was from a different dinosaur. But they kept studying bones and skulls. In 1978, they identified the right skull. It was the one Douglass found. Now Apatosaurus had its real head. Other museums agreed. They asked for copies of the right skull.

The correct skull for Apatosaurus was identified in 1978.

Members of the Sauropod family had long necks with small heads.

Fossil Clues to Study

Apatosaurus was a **sauropod**. Sauropods were a family of dinosaurs. They ate plants. They had long necks with small heads. They walked on land. And they were huge! They were the largest land animals that ever lived. Studying a dinosaur's family can help us learn more about that dinosaur.

Sauropods had small heads. But they ate a lot! They did not chew their food. Scientists have found stones in fossils of sauropod ribs. These stones are called **gastroliths**. Animals swallow them to help grind up food in their stomach. Seals, chickens, and crocodiles do this too.

Scientists think these stones were once in a dinosaur's stomach.

Scientists thought that Apatosaurus's neck was too heavy to lift. They thought its heart was too weak. But now, some think Apatosaurus could stretch up 35 feet (10.7 m)! Its neck bones were partly **hollow**. This made them light. Some scientists think Apatosaurus stood on its hind legs. Then it could reach even higher!

Apatosaurus might have reached branches 35 feet (10.7 m) high.

Apatosaurus Today

We still don't know everything about Apatosaurus. We don't know how it had babies. Scientists think that it laid eggs as big as soccer balls. But Apatosaurus was so tall. Why didn't the eggs break? Scientists have found eggs with leathery skin. This might have kept them safe.

We don't know much about the life of the young Apatosaurus.

27

28

Apatosaurus lived about 140 million years ago. To find its fossils, scientists look in rocks that are this old. Digging for fossils is hard work. But sometimes, scientists find something new. A new fossil. A new bone. Maybe even a new dinosaur! There is always something new to discover when you dig.

There are still more fossils waiting to be discovered.

Glossary

deceptive Having the power to confuse or mislead.

fossil The remains of a plant or animal of a past age preserved in earth or rock.

gastrolith A stone some animals swallow to help them grind food and digest it.

hollow Having empty space inside it.

mosasaur A sea reptile that lived at the time of dinosaurs.

paleontologist A scientist who studies fossils.

sauropod A long-necked, plant-eating dinosaur.

skeleton The frame of bones supporting a body.

spine The backbone, usually made up of many smaller bones.

trackway A series of fossil footprints.

Read More

Bailey, Gerry. *Apatosaurus*. Smithsonian Prehistoric Zone. New York: Crabtree Publishing Company, 2011.

Lessem, Don. *National Geographic Kids Ultimate Dinopedia*. Washington, D.C.: National Geographic, 2010.

Riggs, Kate. *Apatosaurus*. When Dinosaurs Lived. Mankato, Minn.: Creative Paperbacks, 2012.

Websites

Apatosaurus – Enchanted Learning
http://www.enchantedlearning.com/subjects/dinosaurs/dinos/Apatosaurus.shtml

Dinosaurs for Kids – KidsDinos.com
http://www.kidsdinos.com/

Kids Dig Dinos – Dinosaur Facts
http://www.kidsdigdinos.com/dinosaurfacts.htm

Index

About the Author

Barbara Alpert has written 20 children's books and many books for adults. She lives in New York City, where she works as an editor. She loves to travel and has collected fossils in New York, New Jersey, Montana, and Pennsylvania.